GERMANY

Robin Nelson

Lerner Publications Company • Minneapolis

Lerner Publications Company
A division of Lerner Publishing Group, Inc.
241 First Avenue North
Minneapolis, MN 55401 U.S.A.

Website address: www.lernerbooks.com

Library of Congress Cataloging-in-Publication Data

Nelson, Robin, 1971–
    Germany / by Robin Nelson.
        p.   cm. — (Country explorers)
    Includes index.
    ISBN 978–0–7613–6408–5 (lib. bdg. : alk. paper)
    1. Germany—Juvenile literature. I. Title.
  DD17.N37 2011
  943—dc22   2010018956

Manufactured in the United States of America
1 – VI – 12/31/10

Table of Contents

Welcome!

Germany sits on the continent of Europe. The North Sea and the Baltic Sea touch Germany's northern border. In between the seas, Germany borders Denmark. Poland and the Czech Republic lie to the east of Germany. Austria and Switzerland form Germany's southern border. To the west are France, Luxembourg, Belgium, and the Netherlands.

Germany

This Baltic Sea port is in northern Germany.

NORTH
SEA

DENMARK

BALTIC
SEA

POLAND

NORTH FRISIAN ISLANDS

EAST FRISIAN ISLANDS

MILES
0   50   100

0   50   100
KILOMETERS

Hamburg
ELBE RIVER

NORTH GERMAN
PLAIN

Berlin

NETHERLANDS

Cologne
RHINE RIVER

HARZ
MOUNTAINS

GERMANY

ORE
MOUNTAINS

CENTRAL HIGHLANDS

BELGIUM

Frankfurt

CZECH
REPUBLIC

FRANCE

Heidelberg

LUXEMBOURG

NECKAR
RIVER

DANUBE RIVER

RHINE RIVER

Munich

mountains

BLACK FOREST

ZUGSPITZE

country's capital

city

BAVARIAN ALPS

AUSTRIA

SWITZERLAND

The Land

Most of northern Germany is open and flat.
This area is called the North German Plain.

Sheep graze in a field in
the North German Plain.

Hills and valleys cover the land in central Germany. Many rivers and forests run through this part of the country. Mountains and more forests lie to the south.

Map Whiz Quiz

Take a look at the map on page 5. Trace the outline of Germany onto a sheet of paper. Can you find Denmark? Mark this part of your map with an *N* for north. Do you see Poland? Mark it with an *E* for east. How about Switzerland? Mark this side with an *S* for south. Then look for Belgium. Mark it with a *W* for west. Finally, use a blue crayon to trace Germany's rivers.

The Rhine River runs through western Germany.

Zugspitze reaches high into the sky.

Mountains and Trees

Germany's highest mountain is Zugspitze. The mountain is part of the Bavarian Alps. This mountain range runs along Germany's southern border. From the top of Zugspitze, you can see mountaintops in four different countries.

The Black Forest grows near Zugspitze. Trees in the Black Forest grow so close together that it can get very dark in there!

Silver firs thrive in Germany's famous Black Forest.

9

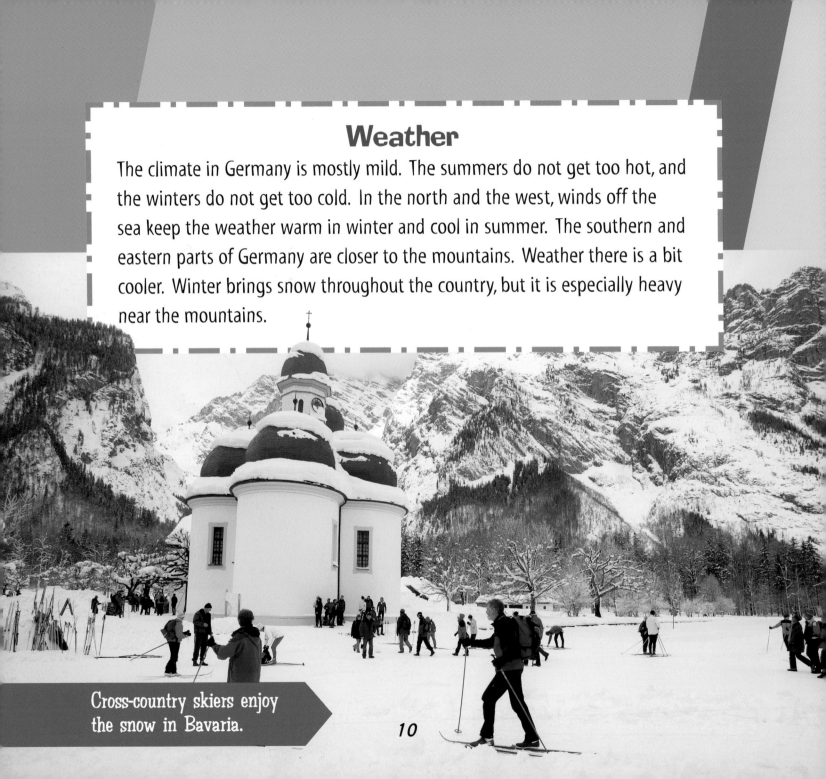

Weather

The climate in Germany is mostly mild. The summers do not get too hot, and the winters do not get too cold. In the north and the west, winds off the sea keep the weather warm in winter and cool in summer. The southern and eastern parts of Germany are closer to the mountains. Weather there is a bit cooler. Winter brings snow throughout the country, but it is especially heavy near the mountains.

Cross-country skiers enjoy the snow in Bavaria.

10

The weather can change quickly in Germany. Sometimes warm air from the north meets cold air from the south. This might cause a thunderstorm in the middle of a sunny summer day!

Lightning flashes over a town in central Germany.

History

Germany is a very old country. People have lived there for more than two thousand years. Germany was a group of states before it became a country. Many European kings and dukes ruled the area. Finally, in 1871, Otto von Bismarck united the different states.

Otto von Bismarck established a new German empire.

Adolf Hitler *(center)* salutes his Nazi troops.

During World War II (1939–1945), the Nazi Party ruled Germany. Adolf Hitler was the Nazi leader. He wanted control of Germany and much of the world. Hitler wanted to get rid of Jews and other groups that he disliked. He put these people in concentration camps. Millions of men, women, and children died in the camps. Some countries knew they had to stop Hitler and the Nazis. These countries attacked, and Germany lost the war.

Two Countries

After World War II, Germany split into two countries. East Germany became a Communist country. The government owned all the land, homes, and businesses. West Germany became a democracy. People there had more freedom.

Berlin is Germany's largest city. Berlin also split into two. The East German government built a wall between East Berlin and West Berlin. The government wanted to stop people from going to West Berlin, the democratic part of the city. The East German government also built fences along the border with West Germany. Guards patrolled the wall and fences. Many families and friends could no longer visit one another.

This wall divided East and West Berlin.

Then, in 1989, East Germany opened its borders. Germans celebrated and tore down the Berlin Wall. On October 3, 1990, East Germany and West Germany became one country again.

People celebrate at the Berlin Wall after East Germany opened its borders in 1989.

Frankfurt is one
of the largest cities
in Germany.

Life in the City

Most people in Germany live in cities or towns. German cities
are busy and exciting! Many cities are filled with very old and
very new buildings. Sometimes the old and new buildings sit
right next to one another.

People walk past the famous Brandenburg Gate.

The Gate to Germany

The Brandenburg Gate is in downtown Berlin. It has come to stand for the city and for Germany. A statue of a goddess and her chariot sits on top of the gate. Four horses are pulling the chariot.

Berlin is the capital of Germany. Workers in Berlin often ride their bikes or take a bus or a train to work. On many streets, no cars are allowed. These streets are only for people to walk along. Berlin is the home to many parks, museums, and old churches.

Life in the Country

Some people in Germany work in the city but live in the country or suburbs. They like to get away from the busy city. Life in the German countryside is quiet and peaceful. Winding streets, old buildings, and markets fill many villages.

A vineyard is the backdrop for this countryside village.

18

Germans living in the country may also work in the country. Some might work on a farm raising animals or crops. Others may live on a vineyard where grapes are grown. Or they might work as shopkeepers, doctors, or business owners.

German Shepherds

German farmers once used German shepherd dogs to help them guard sheep. These dogs are very smart and strong. They are popular pets in Germany and all over the world. Some German shepherds even have jobs working for the police or helping people who have special needs.

This man enjoys a moment with a horse in the Alpine foothills.

Family

Family life is very important in Germany. In many German families, both parents work. Evenings and weekends are for families to spend time together. Many families like to hike, play sports, eat, and play games together.

This family plays games and eats a picnic dinner together.

In the cities, most German families live in their own apartments or smaller houses. In the country, many generations might live together. Children, parents, cousins, uncles, aunts, and grandparents might all live in the same house.

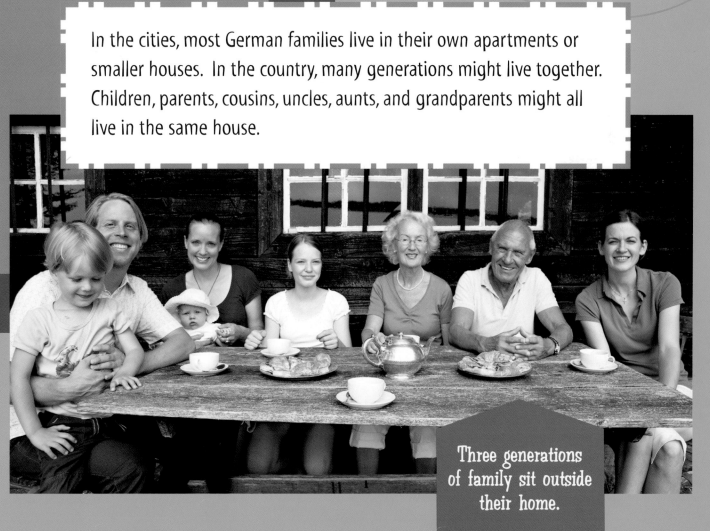

Three generations of family sit outside their home.

Language

The official language of Germany is Hochdeutsch, or High German. Newspapers and TV programs use High German. Plattdeutsch, or Low German, is spoken in northern Germany.

Do you recognize these German words for kiss and dolphin?

Good Words to Know

If you meet a German, here are some good words to know.

hello	hallo	(HA-lo)
good-bye	Auf Wiedersehen	(owf VEE-der-say-en)
yes	ja	(YAH)
no	nein	(NINE)
please	bitte	(BIT-tuh)
thank you	danke	(DAN-kuh)

Köln

Some German words look or sound a lot like English words. *Trinken*, for example, means "to drink." *Apfel* means "apple." And *Haus* means "house."

Some German letters have two dots—called an umlaut—over them. The umlaut changes the sound of the vowel.

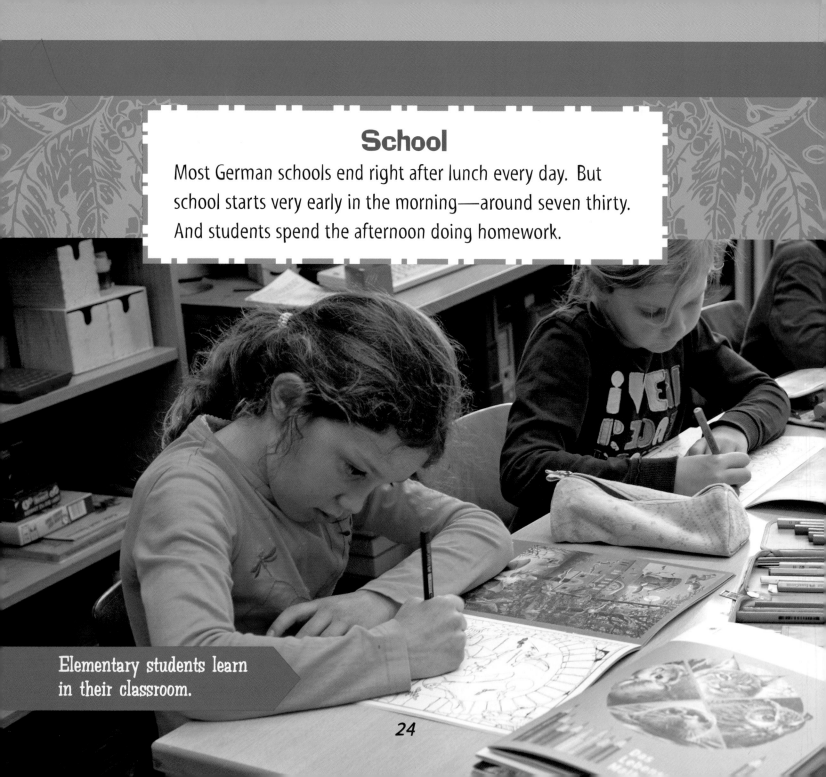

School

Most German schools end right after lunch every day. But school starts very early in the morning—around seven thirty. And students spend the afternoon doing homework.

Elementary students learn in their classroom.

24

Schultuete

Children in Germany start school when they are about six years old. On their first day of school, they get a *Schultuete* from their parents. A Schultuete is a large paper cone filled with candy and school supplies.

Students in Germany get paper cones filled with goodies on the first day of school.

All children go to elementary school. *Grundschule* is for grades one to four. After grade four, students, parents, and teachers choose which type of school students will go to next. Gymnasiums prepare students for college. *Realschule* students study a specific trade or learn skills for a job. Students could also attend a *Hauptschule*, where they learn at a slower pace and prepare for a job.

25

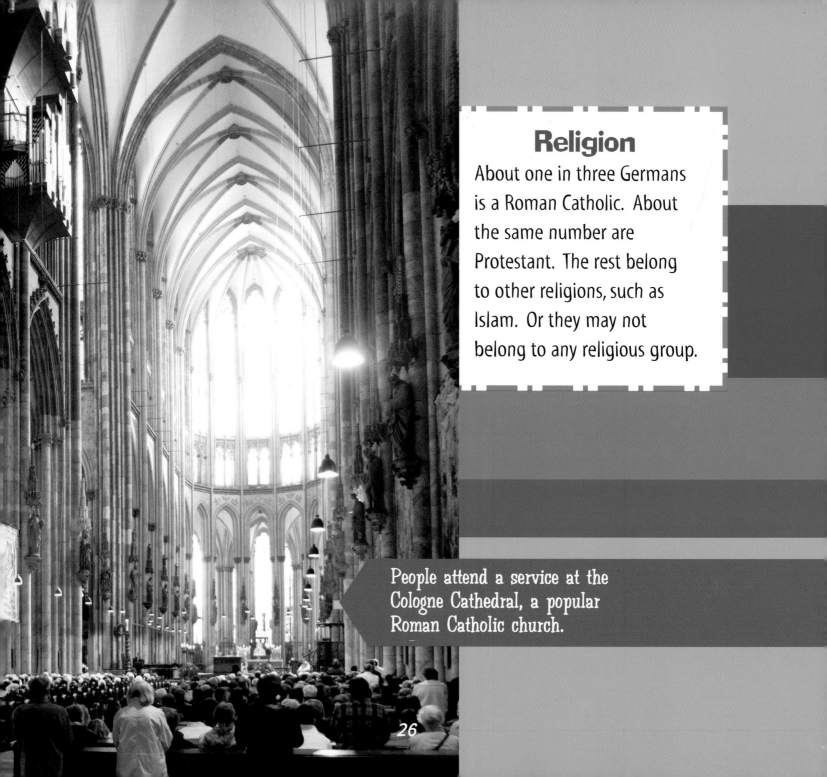

Religion

About one in three Germans is a Roman Catholic. About the same number are Protestant. The rest belong to other religions, such as Islam. Or they may not belong to any religious group.

People attend a service at the Cologne Cathedral, a popular Roman Catholic church.

Martin Luther

Martin Luther was born in Germany in 1483. When he grew up, he became a Catholic priest and teacher. Luther did not agree with everything the Catholic Church said. One day, he wrote down some of the things he disagreed with. A popular story says that he nailed his list to the door of a church. Martin Luther wanted to change the Catholic Church. Instead, he started a new religion. His followers are called Lutherans.

Martin Luther started the Lutheran religion.

Food

Germans enjoy good food. They especially like sausage. They call it wurst. Germany has over 1,500 types of wursts! Germany's wurst even inspired the American hot dog. Have you ever eaten a bratwurst? Then you have eaten a German sausage.

Many types of wursts are displayed in the window of a butcher shop.

Do you like Gummi Bears?

This colorful and yummy candy was first made in Germany! In 1922, a German candymaker invented the Dancing Bear. It was a fruit gum in the shape of a bear. The Gummi Bear became so popular that it inspired other shapes such as worms and other animals.

Every part of Germany has its own way of preparing potatoes. *Knoedels* are dumplings that cooks make in northern Germany. *Spaetzles* are tiny dumplings that cooks make in Southern Germany.

Germans bake hundreds of different kinds of bread. They also enjoy afternoon pastries. Berliners are doughnuts filled with jam and covered with powdered sugar. Yummy!

This Black Forest cake, a southern German dessert, is displayed in a bakery case.

Celebrate!

Oktoberfest is a famous celebration in Germany. Every October, millions of people from all over the world come to Munich to help Germans celebrate! Large tents are put up all over the city. People listen to bands and enjoy food and drinks. Oktoberfest lasts for sixteen days.

Men wearing traditional clothing perform during Oktoberfest.

Germans love to celebrate Christmas. In December, German streets are filled with outdoor markets. Market stalls have handmade toys, decorations, and Christmas treats such as cookies or roasted nuts.

The Christmas celebration starts on Saint Nicholas Day, December 6. The night before, children put one shoe outside the door. In the morning, they find their shoe filled with treats. The tradition of Christmas trees began in Germany. Families decorate the tree and open presents on Christmas Eve. Then they eat dinner and go to church.

People shop at the Munich Christmas market.

The Neuschwanstein Castle is unfinished. Only fourteen rooms are complete.

Castles

Have you ever visited a real castle? Kings, princes, emperors, and dukes built many castles in Germany. Neuschwanstein Castle is one of Germany's most famous. King Ludwig II had builders start work on it in 1869. He spent so much money building castles that people called him Mad King Ludwig. Ludwig moved into Neuschwanstein Castle before it was complete. But he only lived there a few months before he died in 1886.

Cinderella's Castle

The Neuschwanstein Castle in the Bavarian Alps was used as the model for Cinderella's castle in Disney movies and theme parks.

Dear Grandma,

I am having a great time in Germany! Today we took a boat down the Rhine River. First, we went through cities with tall buildings and factories. Then we saw huge cliffs on both sides of the river. There are big, beautiful castles built on some of the cliffs! Long ago, the people in those castles used to collect money from boats that passed by.

See you soon!

Heidi

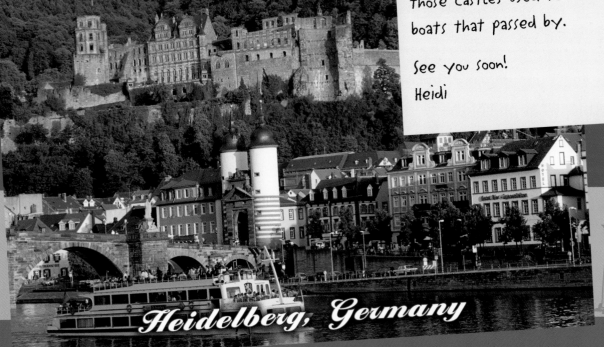

Heidelberg, Germany

A German player (center) tries to keep the ball from two Ghanaian players during the 2010 World Cup.

Sports

The most popular sport in Germany is soccer. Germans call it *Fussball*. Germany has one of the world's best soccer teams. The German team has won the World Cup many times. One of Germany's most famous former soccer players is Gerd Muller. He scored fourteen World Cup goals.

Many German boys and girls play soccer. And even more are fans. Soccer is sometimes called the national sport of Germany because the game is so popular.

Other favorite sports are gymnastics, skiing, snowboarding, handball, and tennis. Some famous tennis stars are from Germany, including Boris Becker and Steffi Graf.

German Steffi Graf plays tennis during the 1994 French Open.

Traveling Fast

Zoom! Many Germans drive fast. Germany built one of the world's first expressways in the 1930s. It is called the Autobahn. The Autobahn is about 7,580 miles (12,200 kilometers) long. It can have up to ten lanes. And it has no speed limit! Drivers can go as fast as they want. But German traffic laws are very strict.

Traffic cruises along the Autobahn.

The Volkswagen Beetle

The Volkswagen Beetle is a very popular car in the United States. The Beetle was first made in Germany in 1938. People call it the Beetle because it is small and shaped like a bug. Volkswagen introduced a new version of the Beetle in 1998.

The original Beetle *(right)* is parked next to the new version of the Beetle *(left).*

Fairy Tales

Did you know that fairy tales about Cinderella, Little Red Riding Hood, and Snow White came from Germany? The brothers Jacob and Wilhelm Grimm collected old German children's stories. The Grimm brothers published their first stories in 1812. People loved them so much that the brothers kept adding more stories. Soon there were more than two hundred tales. *Grimm's Fairy Tales* became some of the most beloved children's stories.

Brothers Jacob and Wilhelm Grimm wrote many of the fairy tales we read.

Brüder Grimm

This book contains a collection of Grimm brothers' fairy tales.

Music

Many famous musicians were born in Germany. Wolfgang Amadeus Mozart began writing music when he was only four years old. Johann Sebastian Bach wrote beautiful music for the organ.

Johann Sebastian Bach is a famous German composer and organist.

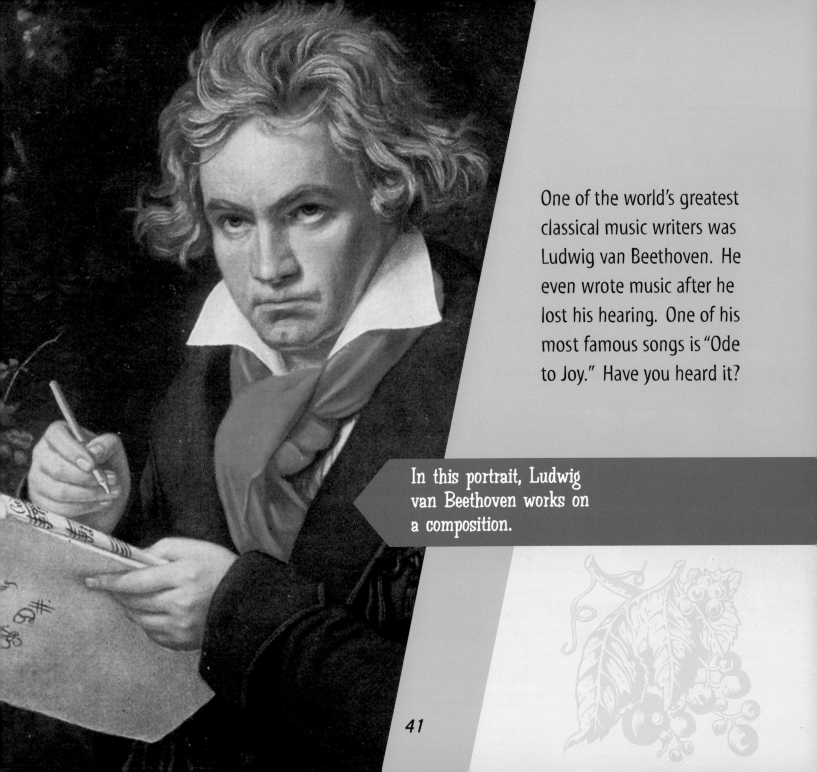

One of the world's greatest classical music writers was Ludwig van Beethoven. He even wrote music after he lost his hearing. One of his most famous songs is "Ode to Joy." Have you heard it?

In this portrait, Ludwig van Beethoven works on a composition.

Jobs

Germany produces many different goods. Cars are one of the most important products. German factories make many kinds of cars. German factories also make machinery, electronics, metals, chemicals, and cloth.

Farmers in Germany grow many crops and raise animals for food. Germany is able to feed almost all its people with its own crops and meat.

People work at a Volkswagen car factory.

Germany uses lots of energy. The country must buy its oil and natural gas from other countries. But German companies are finding new energy sources such as the wind and the sun.

This man makes solar modules that will collect energy from the sun.

THE FLAG OF GERMANY

Germany's flag has three stripes across it. The top stripe is black. The middle stripe is red. And the bottom stripe is gold. These colors have been linked with German unity since the 1800s. The flag was first used in 1849. It became the national flag in 1919 and remained so until 1933. In 1949, it was permanently adopted as the national flag.

FAST FACTS

FULL COUNTRY NAME: Federal Republic of Germany

AREA: 137,847 square miles (357,021 square kilometers), or a little smaller than the state of Montana

MAIN LANDFORMS: the mountain ranges Bavarian Alps, Harz, and Ore; the Central Highlands; the North German Plain; the coastal lowlands

MAJOR RIVERS: Rhine, Elbe, Danube

ANIMALS AND THEIR HABITATS: gray seals (coast); beavers, deer, grouse, lynx, wild boar (forests); chamois, ibex (mountains); badgers, foxes, polecats (central hills); fish (rivers, lakes, North Sea, and Baltic Sea)

CAPITAL CITY: Berlin

OFFICIAL LANGUAGE: High German

POPULATION: about 82,283,000

GLOSSARY

capital: a city where the government of a state or a country is located

concentration camps: places where the Nazis held Jews and other prisoners. Millions of people died in these camps during World War II.

continent: any one of seven large areas of land. The continents are Africa, Antarctica, Asia, Australia, Europe, North America, and South America.

map: a drawing or chart of all or part of Earth or the sky

mountain: a part of Earth's surface that rises high into the sky

vineyard: a field where grapevines grow

TO LEARN MORE

BOOKS

Landau, Elaine. *German Shepherds Are the Best!* Minneapolis: Lerner Publications Company, 2010. Discover more about this wonderful breed that got its start in Germany.

Parnell, Helga. *Cooking the German Way.* Minneapolis: Lerner Publications Company, 2003. Learn how to cook traditional German food the easy way.

Simmons, Walter. *Germany.* Minneapolis: Bellwether Media, 2010. Learn more about German culture and history.

WEBSITES

Country Reports Germany
http://www.countryreports.org/country.aspx?countryid=91&countryName=Germany
This site is filled with information kids need for country reports.

German Missions in the United States
http://www.germany.info/Vertretung/usa/en/Startseite.html
This website from the German Embassy has a section for kids and teens.

National Geographic Germany
http://kids.nationalgeographic.com/Places/Find/Germany
Watch videos, look at maps, send an e-card, and more on this site from *National Geographic.*

Time for Kids Around the World: Germany
http://www.timeforkids.com/TFK/teachers/aw/wr/main/0,28132,1147387,00.html
This site includes a sightseeing guide, native lingo, and games about Germany.

INDEX